Writing

My Story

Writing

My Story

A Journaling Guide for Kids

MAISHA MCGEE-CHILDS

tate publishing

CHILDREN'S DIVISION

Published by Tate Publishing & Enterprises, LLC
127 E. Trade Center Terrace | Mustang, Oklahoma 73064 USA
1.888.361.9473 | www.tatepublishing.com

Tate Publishing is committed to excellence in the publishing industry. The company reflects the philosophy established by the founders, based on Psalm 68:11,
"The Lord gave the word and great was the company of those who published it."

Book design copyright © 2012 by Tate Publishing, LLC. All rights reserved.
Cover and interior design by Chris Webb
Illustrations by Greg White

Published in the United States of America

ISBN: 978-1-61346-991-0
Juvenile Nonfiction / Language Arts / Composition & Creative Writing
12.01.10

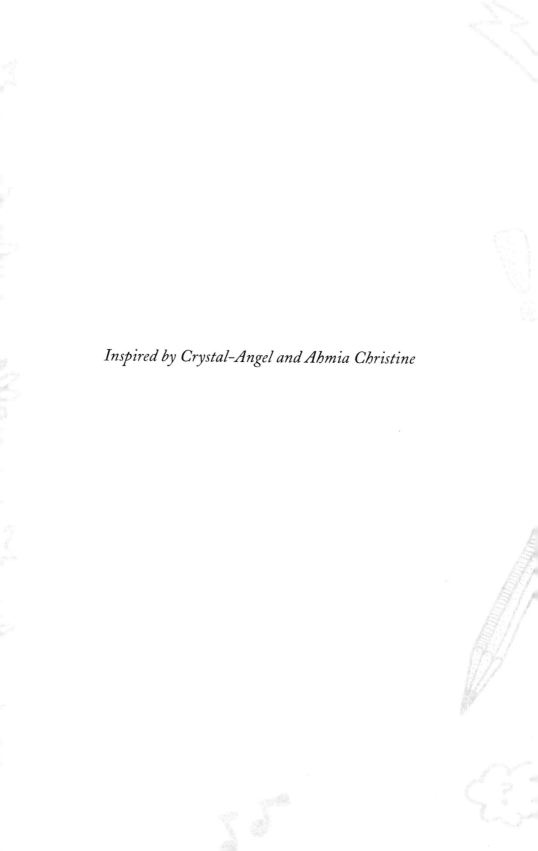

Inspired by Crystal–Angel and Ahmia Christine

This book was presented to:

_____

On:

_____

By:

_____

Place Photo Here

Table of Contents

Facts about Me

For he chose us in him before the creation of the
world to be holy and blameless in his sight.
Ephesians—1:4 NIV

My name means:

_____

My birthday is:

_____

I was born on a:

_____

at_____am/pm

My favorite color is:

_____

The best things about me are:

_____

What every person should know about me:

_____

_____

Today's date:

_____

Today I am feeling:

_____

The best part of my day was:

_____

Today I learned:

_____

Today I want to pray for:

_____

I thank God today for:

_____

Tomorrow I will do the following:

_____

I Am a Child of God

Don't let anyone look down on you because you are young, but set an example for the believers in speech, in life, in love, in faith and in purity.
1 Timothy 4:12 NIV

I interpret this scripture to mean:

_____

_____

_____

_____

_____

I set daily examples that I am a child of God by:

_____

_____

_____

_____

This is what happened in my life today:

_____

_____

Today's date:

_____

Today I am feeling:

_____

The best part of my day was:

_____

Today I learned:

_____

Today I want to pray for:

_____

I thank God today for:

_____

Tomorrow I will do the following:

_____

God is Guiding Me to be Brilliant

I will instruct you and teach you in the way you should go; I will counsel you and watch over you. Psalm 32:8 NIV

I think being brilliant means:

_____

_____

_____

The brilliant people I admire for changing the world and/or my life are:

_____

_____

_____

I am brilliant and motivate people in the following ways:

_____

_____

_____

This is what happened in my life today:

_____

_____

Today's date:

_____

Today I am feeling:

_____

The best part of my day was:

_____

Today I learned:

_____

Today I want to pray for:

_____

I thank God today for:

_____

Tomorrow I will do the following:

_____

School

For everything that was written in the past was written to teach us, so that through endurance and the encouragement of the Scriptures we might have hope.
Romans 15:4 NIV

The school I attend is called:

_____

My best friends are:

_____

When I'm with my friends we love to:

_____

The thing I'd like to change most about my school is:

_____

My favorite thing to do at school is:

_____

My favorite subject is:

_____

What I love most about my school is:

_____

My favorite teachers are:

_____

Today's date:

_____

Today I am feeling:

_____

The best part of my day was:

_____

Today I learned:

_____

Today I want to pray for:

_____

I thank God today for:

_____

Tomorrow I will do the following:

_____

If I Could Change
a Day of School

Let the wise hear and increase in learning, and the one who understands
obtain guidance.
Proverbs 1:5 ESV

This is what my most embarrassing day at school was like:

_____

_____

I wish I could replace my worst day ever with a new day. Maybe even a day as the school principal. If I were the principal I would change the following rules:

_____

_____

I would want the teachers to run their classrooms this way:

_____

_____

_____

This is what happened in my life today:

_____

_____

Today's date:

_____

Today I am feeling:

_____

The best part of my day was:

_____

Today I learned:

_____

Today I want to pray for:

_____

I thank God today for:

_____

Tomorrow I will do the following:

_____

I Honor My Parents

Honor your father and your mother, so that you may live long in the land the Lord your God is giving you.
Exodus 20:12 NIV

I honor my parents daily by:

_____

_____

_____

I will continue to honor my parents as an adult when I:

_____

_____

_____

I would like my children to honor me by:

_____

_____

_____

This is what happened in my life today:

_____

_____

_____

Today's date:

_____

Today I am feeling:

_____

The best part of my day was:

_____

Today I learned:

_____

Today I want to pray for:

_____

I thank God today for:

_____

Tomorrow I will do the following:

_____

Gifts from God

Every good gift and every perfect gift is from above,
coming down from the Father of lights with whom there is
no variation or shadow due to change.
James 1:17 ESV

I know I am beautiful/handsome because:

_____

_____

I am smart because:

_____

_____

My talents are:

_____

_____

The things my family loves the most about me are:

_____

_____

This is what happened in my life today:

_____

_____

Today's date:

_____

Today I am feeling:

_____

The best part of my day was:

_____

Today I learned:

_____

Today I want to pray for:

_____

I thank God today for:

_____

Tomorrow I will do the following:

_____

A Poem About My Strength and Character

I can do all things through him who strengthens me.
Psalms 4:13 NIV

A poem about me would sound like this:

_____

_____

_____

_____

_____

_____

_____

_____

_____

_____

_____

_____

_____

_____

Today's date:

_____

Today I am feeling:

_____

The best part of my day was:

_____

Today I learned:

_____

Today I want to pray for:

_____

I thank God today for:

_____

Tomorrow I will do the following:

_____

I Am Focused on Making My Dreams Come True

Trust in the Lord with all your heart and lean
not on your own understanding;
Proverbs 3:5 NIV

These are the things I am doing to help make my dreams come true:

_____

_____

_____

My top two goals I want to accomplish this year are:

_____

_____

My top five goals I want to accomplish in life are:

_____

_____

_____

_____

_____

This is what happened in my life today:

_____

_____

Today's date:

_____

Today I am feeling:

_____

The best part of my day was:

_____

Today I learned:

_____

Today I want to pray for:

_____

I thank God today for:

_____

Tomorrow I will do the following:

_____

God Is Always With Me

So do not fear, for I am with you; do not be dismayed,
for I am your God. I will strengthen you and help you; I
will uphold you with my righteous right hand."
Isaiah 41:10 NIV

The times I have been really afraid, I did this to overcome my fear:

_____

_____

_____

_____

The things I am sometimes afraid of are:

_____

_____

_____

This is what I do to overcome my current fears:

_____

_____

_____

This is what happened in my life today:

_____

_____

Today's date:

_____

Today I am feeling:

_____

The best part of my day was:

_____

Today I learned:

_____

Today I want to pray for:

_____

I thank God today for:

_____

Tomorrow I will do the following:

_____

God Promises to Answer My Prayers

You may ask for anything in my name, and I will do it.
John 14:14 NIV

I would like to ask God in the name of His Son Jesus Christ to answer this prayer for me:

_____

_____

_____

_____

_____

I would like to request that God in the name of His Son Jesus Christ answer the following prayer for the person named below:

_____

_____

_____

_____

_____

This is what happened in my life today:

_____

_____

Today's date:

_____

Today I am feeling:

_____

The best part of my day was:

_____

Today I learned:

_____

Today I want to pray for:

_____

I thank God today for:

_____

Tomorrow I will do the following:

_____

I Appreciate My Teachers and Parents

First, I thank my God through Jesus Christ for all of you, because your faith is being reported all over the world.
Romans 1:8 NIV

I know just how special my principal and teachers really are. I want to thank the principal and my teachers for:

_____

_____

_____

_____

_____

_____

_____

_____

_____

_____

_____

_____

_____

Today's date:

_____

Today I am feeling:

_____

The best part of my day was:

_____

Today I learned:

_____

Today I want to pray for:

_____

I thank God today for:

_____

Tomorrow I will do the following:

_____

Favorites

Book

_____

Movie

_____

Actor

_____

Singer

_____

Band

_____

TV Show

_____

Restaurant

_____

Foods

_____

Saying

_____

Today's date:

_____

Today I am feeling:

_____

The best part of my day was:

_____

Today I learned:

_____

Today I want to pray for:

_____

I thank God today for:

_____

Tomorrow I will do the following:

_____

I Love Learning New Things

We have different gifts, according to the grace given us.
Romans 12:6 NIV

The new things I learned last year were:

_____

_____

_____

_____

I have incorporated the new things I learned last year into making me a better person this year by:

_____

_____

_____

The new things I want to learn this year are:

_____

_____

_____

This is what happened in my life today:

_____

_____

Today's date:

_____

Today I am feeling:

_____

The best part of my day was:

_____

Today I learned:

_____

Today I want to pray for:

_____

I thank God today for:

_____

Tomorrow I will do the following:

_____

I Love Myself

So God created man in his own image, in the image of God he created him;
male and female he created them.
Genesis 1:27 ESV

The things I love most about myself are:

_____

_____

_____

_____

_____

_____

I thank God for creating me in his image to be able to do:

_____

_____

_____

_____

_____

_____

This is what happened in my life today:

_____

_____

Today's date:

_____

Today I am feeling:

_____

The best part of my day was:

_____

Today I learned:

_____

Today I want to pray for:

_____

I thank God today for:

_____

Tomorrow I will do the following:

_____

God is a Forgiving God

*If we confess our sins, he is faithful and just and will forgive us our sins
and purify us from all unrighteousness.*
1 John 1:9 NIV

I ask God forgiveness for doing:

_____

_____

_____

_____

_____

_____

I know God will forgive me of my past sins because:

_____

_____

_____

_____

_____

_____

This is what happened in my life today:

_____

_____

Today's date:

_____

Today I am feeling:

_____

The best part of my day was:

_____

Today I learned:

_____

Today I want to pray for:

_____

I thank God today for:

_____

Tomorrow I will do the following:

_____

Dreams

When I grow up I want to be:

_____

I am afraid of:

_____

I have a secret crush on:

_____

If I could meet one person from heaven, it would be:

_____

If I could meet one famous person, it would be:

_____

The one place in the world I would like to go is:

_____

Today's date:

_____

Today I am feeling:

_____

The best part of my day was:

_____

Today I learned:

_____

Today I want to pray for:

_____

I thank God today for:

_____

Tomorrow I will do the following:

_____

What's...

Hot! _____

Not! _____

Who...

Is cool! _____

Do I want to throw in a pool! _____

I Wish...

I never: _____

I could: _____

I Will...

Be: _____

Go: _____

Achieve: _____

Today's date:

_____

Today I am feeling:

_____

The best part of my day was:

_____

Today I learned:

_____

Today I want to pray for:

_____

I thank God today for:

_____

Tomorrow I will do the following:

_____

I Love Life

For God so loved the world, that he gave his only begotten Son, that who-soever believeth in him should not perish, but have everlasting life.
John 3:16 KJV

What I love most about my life is:

_____

_____

_____

_____

_____

_____

I wish I could change the following about my life:

_____

_____

_____

_____

_____

_____

This is what happened in my life today:

_____

_____

Today's date:

_____

Today I am feeling:

_____

The best part of my day was:

_____

Today I learned:

_____

Today I want to pray for:

_____

I thank God today for:

_____

Tomorrow I will do the following:

_____

I Can Accomplish Anything

I can do everything through him who gives me strength.
Philippians 4:13 NIV

I am most proud of accomplishing the following this year in school:

_____

_____

I am most proud of accomplishing the following in sports, art, and/or music:

_____

_____

I would like to improve on:

_____

_____

I will accomplish these things next year:

_____

_____

This is what happened in my life today:

_____

_____

Today's date:

_____

Today I am feeling:

_____

The best part of my day was:

_____

Today I learned:

_____

Today I want to pray for:

_____

I thank God today for:

_____

Tomorrow I will do the following:

_____

I Love Others Just as Christ Loves Me

I have told you this so that my joy may be in you and that your joy may be complete. My command is this: Love each other as I have loved you. Greater love has no one than this, that he lay down his life for his friends.
John 15: 11-13 NIV

I show my love and appreciation for my friends by:

_____

_____

_____

_____

I show my love and appreciation for my family by:

_____

_____

_____

_____

My family shows love and appreciation for me by:

_____

_____

_____

_____

I show love for strangers by:

_____

_____

_____

_____

I show love and forgiveness for people that have hurt me by:

_____

_____

_____

_____

This is what I did in my life today:

_____

_____

A perfect day from the time I awake until bedtime would be:

Today is the day the LORD has made; let us rejoice and be glad in it.
Psalm 118:24 NIV

_____

_____

_____

_____

_____

_____

_____

_____

_____

_____

_____

_____

_____

_____

Today's date:

_____

Today I am feeling:

_____

The best part of my day was:

_____

Today I learned:

_____

Today I want to pray for:

_____

I thank God today for:

_____

Tomorrow I will do the following:

_____

More About Me

Before I formed you in the womb I knew you,
before you were born I set you apart.
Jeremiah. 1:5

I am most annoyed by:

_____

My most embarrassing moment was:

_____

I get emotional when:

_____

_____ makes me happy.

_____makes me sad.

I don't stay sad long because _____always cheers me up!

This is what happened in my life today:

_____

_____

Today's date:

_____

Today I am feeling:

_____

The best part of my day was:

_____

Today I learned:

_____

Today I want to pray for:

_____

I thank God today for:

_____

Tomorrow I will do the following:

_____

The 23rd Psalm

The Lord is my shepherd, I shall not want. He makes me lie down in green pastures, he leads me beside quiet waters, he restores my soul. He guides me in paths of righteousness for his name's sake. Even though I walk through the valley of the shadow of death, I will fear no evil, for you are with me; your rod and your staff, they do comfort me. You prepare a table before me in the presence of my enemies. You anoint my head with oil; my cup over-flows. Surely goodness and love will follow me all the days of my life, and I will dwell in the house of the Lord forever.

I will memorize this bible verse and repeat it to myself when I feel afraid. I will believe that God is with me and will protect me.

This is what I did one time when I was really afraid:

_____

_____

_____

_____

_____

_____

_____

This is what happened in my life today:

_____

_____

Today's date:

_____

Today I am feeling:

_____

The best part of my day was:

_____

Today I learned:

_____

Today I want to pray for:

_____

I thank God today for:

_____

Tomorrow I will do the following:

_____

Jesus Walks With Me

It's normal to be afraid but I will never let fear make me give up. I will pray to God when I feel alone, scared, or nervous and remember that He is always with me. If I fail at something, I will not be discouraged but I will have faith that I will do better next time.

This short story is about a time when I failed at something and then worked harder the next time to be successful. This is what I did differently the second time around:

_____

_____

_____

_____

_____

_____

_____

_____

_____

_____

Today's date:

_____

Today I am feeling:

_____

The best part of my day was:

_____

Today I learned:

_____

Today I want to pray for:

_____

I thank God today for:

_____

Tomorrow I will do the following:

_____

I Appreciate the People that Love and Help Me

...May the Lord reward you for your kindness...
Ruth 1:8 NLT

My parents show they love me by:

_____

_____

_____

My friends show they love me by:

_____

_____

_____

My siblings and other relatives show they love me by:

_____

_____

_____

My teachers show they love me by:

_____

_____

_____

A stranger has gone out of their way to show me they care about me by:

_____

_____

_____

I would you show a pet that I love them by:

_____

_____

_____

This is what happened in my life today:

_____

_____

Today's date:

_____

Today I am feeling:

_____

The best part of my day was:

_____

Today I learned:

_____

Today I want to pray for:

_____

I thank God today for:

_____

Tomorrow I will do the following:

_____

My Talents Make Me Wealthy

This is a day in the life of me as the Boss!

Good morning, everyone! I am excited to see my entire staff here at _____(name of the business you own).

Today we will be working on finishing: _____

_____(project you and your staff are working on).

I am leaving early because I am moving into my dream house in

_____ (state, country).

I will need you all to handle everything while I am gone. Tomorrow you are all invited to a house warming party to help me celebrate the purchase of my new _____

(beach house, country castle, condo, town house, cabin, etc.)!

We will all be dancing to_____ (favorite type of music)

and wearing _____(favorite type of clothes)

with _____(favorite type of shoes).

We will be eating all the _____ (favorite desert)

you can stand and drinking all the _____(favorite soda)

your somach can handle!

Everyone will have to know how to do the_____(favorite dance) and you will be video taped!

I ask all the ladies to wear a_____(favorite flower) in their hair and all the guys to wear a _____ (favorite sports team) baseball cap.

After we dance we will go outside to play _____ (favorite sport).

The winning team will all get _____ (gift you'd like to receive).

Can't wait to see you there! My house will be the one with the _____(favorite color) (dream car) in the driveway.

Today's date:

_____

Today I am feeling:

_____

The best part of my day was:

_____

Today I learned:

_____

Today I want to pray for:

_____

I thank God today for:

_____

Tomorrow I will do the following:

_____

My Body Is Perfect for Me

You are altogether beautiful, my love; there is no flaw in you.
Song of Solomon 4:7 ESV

Everyone is different inside and out, yet God made everyone unique and special. This is what is unique and special about my face:

_____

_____

_____

_____

_____

_____

This is what I love about my body:

_____

_____

_____

_____

_____

_____

This is what happened in my life today:

_____

_____

Today's date:

_____

Today I am feeling:

_____

The best part of my day was:

_____

Today I learned:

_____

Today I want to pray for:

_____

I thank God today for:

_____

Tomorrow I will do the following:

_____

Forgiveness Will Set Me Free

*Be kind to one another, tenderhearted, forgiving one another,
even as God in Christ forgave you.*
Ephesians 4:32 (NIV)

In this letter I apologize to all I have been unkind to. I now understand that God will forgive me when He knows I am sincerely sorry and I am working my hardest to treat people the way I want to be treated.

Dear _____

_____

_____

_____

_____

_____

_____

_____

_____

Sincerely,

_____

Today's date:

_____

Today I am feeling:

_____

The best part of my day was:

_____

Today I learned:

_____

Today I want to pray for:

_____

I thank God today for:

_____

Tomorrow I will do the following:

_____

Comedian

The funniest joke I ever heard was:

_____

_____

_____

_____

_____

I know I'm funny, and I can draw too. If I were making a comic strip, this is what I'd do!

Today's date:

_____

Today I am feeling:

_____

The best part of my day was:

_____

Today I learned:

_____

Today I want to pray for:

_____

I thank God today for:

_____

Tomorrow I will do the following:

_____

I Define Myself

See what kind of love the Father has given to us, that we
should be called children of God: and so we are. The reason why
the world does not know us is that it did not know him.
1John 3:1 ESV

This is how I define myself:

_____

_____

_____

Some people have thought untrue things about me like:

_____

_____

_____

I would like people to see me as:

_____

_____

_____

This is what happened in my life today:

_____

_____

Today's date:

_____

Today I am feeling:

_____

The best part of my day was:

_____

Today I learned:

_____

Today I want to pray for:

_____

I thank God today for:

_____

Tomorrow I will do the following:

_____

My Parents are Smarter than I Think

Listen to your father's instruction and do not forsake your mother's teaching.
Proverbs 1:8 (NIV)

My parents were my age once and have experienced almost everything I will go through. I may not always want to obey my parents, but they know what is best for me.

I just wish my parents understood these things better about me:

_____

_____

_____

_____

_____

_____

I will try harder at these things so my parents won't get upset with me sometimes:

_____

_____

_____

_____

_____

Today's date:

_____

Today I am feeling:

_____

The best part of my day was:

_____

Today I learned:

_____

Today I want to pray for:

_____

I thank God today for:

_____

Tomorrow I will do the following:

_____

I Praise the Lord Daily

God demonstrates His own love toward us,
in that while we were still sinners, Christ died for us.
Romans 5:8 NIV

Jesus Christ died so we can be forgiven of our sins. This is how I show my love for Jesus:

_____

_____

I am still angry with someone who has hurt me but I know I should forgive him/her like Jesus forgives me.

I will release myself from resentment by forgiving them in this short letter:

Dear _____

_____

_____

_____

_____

_____

_____

Sincerely,

_____

Today's date:

_____

Today I am feeling:

_____

The best part of my day was:

_____

Today I learned:

_____

Today I want to pray for:

_____

I thank God today for:

_____

Tomorrow I will do the following:

_____

I Might Be a Singer/ Songwriter or Rapper

Here is a song/rap about me:

_____

_____

_____

_____

_____

_____

_____

_____

_____

_____

_____

_____

_____

_____

_____

_____

Today's date:

_____

Today I am feeling:

_____

The best part of my day was:

_____

Today I learned:

_____

Today I want to pray for:

_____

I thank God today for:

_____

Tomorrow I will do the following:

_____

Lights, Camera, Action!

With all of my talent, I might want to be a movie star or a film producer! I would star in a movie about _____

and if I wrote and directed a movie this is what it would be about:

Characters:

_____

Place:

_____

Time (past, present, or future):

_____

The story goes like this:

_____

_____

_____

_____

_____

_____

_____

_____

Today's date:

_____

Today I am feeling:

_____

The best part of my day was:

_____

Today I learned:

_____

Today I want to pray for:

_____

I thank God today for:

_____

Tomorrow I will do the following:

_____

It Is Easy for Me to Make Friends

My command is this: Love each other as I have loved you. Greater love has no one than this, that he lay down his life for his friends.
John 15:12-13 NIV

What do you love most about making new friends?

_____

_____

_____

_____

Have you ever been scared that you wouldn't make friends somewhere and one of your best friends now helped you to fit in? What did he/she do to help you fit in?

_____

_____

_____

_____

_____

This is what happened in my life today:

_____

_____

Today's date:

_____

Today I am feeling:

_____

The best part of my day was:

_____

Today I learned:

_____

Today I want to pray for:

_____

I thank God today for:

_____

Tomorrow I will do the following:

_____

Have Faith in All I Do

Commit to the Lord whatever you do, and your plans will succeed.
Proverbs 16:3 (NIV)

These are my current plans for this weekend:

_____

_____

These are my plans for this summer:

_____

_____

_____

I understand that not only are my parents watching me but God is watching me. This is how I plan to be the best I can be in my exciting project, music, or dance recital I have coming up. I know God and my parents will be very proud.

_____

_____

_____

_____

This is what happened in my life today:

_____

_____

Today's date:

_____

Today I am feeling:

_____

The best part of my day was:

_____

Today I learned:

_____

Today I want to pray for:

_____

I thank God today for:

_____

Tomorrow I will do the following:

_____

I Respect Myself and Others

Do to others as you would have them do to you.
Luke 6:31 NIV

It is always important to be kind and helpful to others. Respect other people's feelings, ideas, and talents. These are the ways I respect others daily:

_____

_____

_____

People respect me in these ways:

_____

_____

_____

This is how I respect my mind and body:

_____

_____

_____

This is what happened in my life today:

_____

_____

Today's date:

_____

Today I am feeling:

_____

The best part of my day was:

_____

Today I learned:

_____

Today I want to pray for:

_____

I thank God today for:

_____

Tomorrow I will do the following:

_____

I Can't Put This Book Down!

I might decide to be an author. If I wrote a book about my best

friend or siblings, I would change _____'s name to

_____(nickname).

I would write about all the things I love about my friends or sib-

lings like: _____, and I would change the

annoying things my friends/siblings do like: _____.

I might include a mysterious_____(favorite animal)

that eats _____ (favorite candy)

and develops super powers.

The _____(name of animal with super powers)

would ride on a _____(favoite thing with wheels)

and live on the planet _____.

Today's date:

_____

Today I am feeling:

_____

The best part of my day was:

_____

Today I learned:

_____

Today I want to pray for:

_____

I thank God today for:

_____

Tomorrow I will do the following:

_____

Here is the first chapter of my book:

_____

_____

_____

_____

_____

_____

_____

_____

_____

_____

_____

_____

_____

_____

_____

_____

Today's date:

_____

Today I am feeling:

_____

The best part of my day was:

_____

Today I learned:

_____

Today I want to pray for:

_____

I thank God today for:

_____

Tomorrow I will do the following:

_____

I Am a Leader

Whoever walks with the wise grows wise,
but the companion of fools will suffer harm.
Proverbs 13:20 NIV

This is how I show leadership at home:

_____

_____

_____

This is how I show leadership at school?

_____

_____

_____

I will be a leader when I grow up and these are the changes I will make to help make the world a better place:

_____

_____

_____

This is what happened in my life today:

_____

_____

Today's date:

_____

Today I am feeling:

_____

The best part of my day was:

_____

Today I learned:

_____

Today I want to pray for:

_____

I thank God today for:

_____

Tomorrow I will do the following:

_____

My Family Knows That I Am Special

I praise you because I am fearfully and wonderfully made;
Psalms 138:14

I am unique and special from other children in these ways:

_____

_____

_____

I am special to my family in the following ways:

_____

_____

_____

My family lets me know they appreciate me just the way I am by:

_____

_____

_____

This is what happened in my today:

_____

_____

Today's date:

_____

Today I am feeling:

_____

The best part of my day was:

_____

Today I learned:

_____

Today I want to pray for:

_____

I thank God today for:

_____

Tomorrow I will do the following:

_____

My Faith in God Helps Me to Achieve

And without faith it is impossible to please God,
because anyone who comes to him must believe that he exists
and that he rewards those who earnestly seek him.
Hebrews 11:6 (NIV)

I have shown faith in God in the past by:

_____

_____

_____

I show faith in God daily by:

_____

_____

_____

My family shows faith in God by:

_____

_____

_____

This is what happened in my life today:

_____

_____

Today's date:

_____

Today I am feeling:

_____

The best part of my day was:

_____

Today I learned:

_____

Today I want to pray for:

_____

I thank God today for:

_____

Tomorrow I will do the following:

_____

Design, Cut, Sew!

I love clothes but my personal favorites are:

Flip flops, boots, tennis shoes, or dress shoes: _____

Type of hats: _____

Warm up suit or jeans: _____

Dress or suit: _____

Dress shirt or T shirt: _____

Tight clothes or loose: _____

Long hair or short hair: _____

Skinny jeans or bootleg: _____

Uniform or free dress: _____

Today's date:

_____

Today I am feeling:

_____

The best part of my day was:

_____

Today I learned:

_____

Today I want to pray for:

_____

I thank God today for:

_____

Tomorrow I will do the following:

_____

These Are My Designs:

Shirt

Dress

Pants

Coat

Business Suit

Boots

Swimsuit/Swim trunks

Today's date:

_____

Today I am feeling:

_____

The best part of my day was:

_____

Today I learned:

_____

Today I want to pray for:

_____

I thank God today for:

_____

Tomorrow I will do the following:

_____

I Stand up for Myself

A wise man is full of strength, and a man of knowledge enhances his might.
Proverbs 24:5 NIV

Although it is important to respect people's feelings, it is also important for people to respect my feelings. I am strong and stand up for myself when someone tries to hurt me or does something I don't appreciate. I will tell my parents and teachers right away if I ever feel threatened in any kind of way.

I have stood up for myself in this way in the past:

_____

_____

_____

_____

_____

This story is about a child that was bullied and how the child finally stood up for him or herself:

_____

_____

_____

_____

_____

Today's date:

_____

Today I am feeling:

_____

The best part of my day was:

_____

Today I learned:

_____

Today I want to pray for:

_____

I thank God today for:

_____

Tomorrow I will do the following:

_____

I Am Not Afraid When I trust in the Lord

The Lord is my light and my salvation—whom shall I fear?
Psalm 27:1 (NIV)

This is what I would do if one of my friends were bullying someone else:

_____

_____

_____

_____

_____

The reasons I would never bully someone are:

_____

_____

_____

_____

_____

This is what happened in my life today:

_____

_____

_____

Today's date:

_____

Today I am feeling:

_____

The best part of my day was:

_____

Today I learned:

_____

Today I want to pray for:

_____

I thank God today for:

_____

Tomorrow I will do the following:

_____

I Display Love by Encouraging and Supporting My Friends and Family

Whoever does not love does not know God, because God is love.
1John 4:8 NIV

It is important to encourage and support my friends at school and in sports.

I encourage my friends in the following ways at school:

_____

_____

_____

_____

This is how I encourage family members:

_____

_____

_____

In this story I am playing in a championship game and this is how my team displayed unconditional love for me:

_____

_____

Today's date:

_____

Today I am feeling:

_____

The best part of my day was:

_____

Today I learned:

_____

Today I want to pray for:

_____

I thank God today for:

_____

Tomorrow I will do the following:

_____

It's Fun Being a Kid

I had the most fun ever at:

_____

_____

I love it when I get to do:

_____

_____

I love when my mom, dad, grandma, or grandpa does:

_____

Secretly, I still love going to:

_____

_____

Secretly, I still love doing:

_____

_____

I can't believe I ever did:

_____

_____

Today's date:

_____

Today I am feeling:

_____

The best part of my day was:

_____

Today I learned:

_____

Today I want to pray for:

_____

I thank God today for:

_____

Tomorrow I will do the following:

_____

Mom or Dad For a Day

If I could be my mom or dad for a day, the first thing I would do differently at home would be

_____

_____

There would be no more _____ and much more _____.

This is how I would run the house from sun up to sun down:

_____

_____

_____

_____

_____

_____

_____

_____

_____

_____

_____

Today's date:

_____

Today I am feeling:

_____

The best part of my day was:

_____

Today I learned:

_____

Today I want to pray for:

_____

I thank God today for:

_____

Tomorrow I will do the following:

_____

Mom or Dad for a Day

At the end of the day, I would want my parents to understand this about me.

_____

_____

_____

Even though I might do things different from my mom or dad, I love these things about them very much:

_____

_____

_____

Today I want to thank my parents for:

_____

Here is a picture of my family:

Today's date:

_____

Today I am feeling:

_____

The best part of my day was:

_____

Today I learned:

_____

Today I want to pray for:

_____

I thank God today for:

_____

Tomorrow I will do the following:

_____

Beauty is in the Eye of the Beholder

The Lord doesn't see things the way you see them. People judge by outward appearances, but the Lord looks at the heart."
1 Samuel 16:7 (NLT)

I will try not to judge another person based on their appearance but get to know them instead. I remember a time when I judged someone unfairly and found out they were nothing like I had expected. Here is what happened:

_____

_____

_____

_____

_____

_____

_____

_____

_____

This is what happened in my life today:

_____

_____

Today's date:

_____

Today I am feeling:

_____

The best part of my day was:

_____

Today I learned:

_____

Today I want to pray for:

_____

I thank God today for:

_____

Tomorrow I will do the following:

_____

I Am a Songwriter

Worship the Lord with gladness; come before him with joyful songs.
Psalm 100:2 (NIV)

If I were writing a song to the Lord, this is what I would write:

_____

_____

_____

_____

_____

_____

_____

_____

_____

_____

_____

This is what happened in my life today:

_____

_____

Today's date:

_____

Today I am feeling:

_____

The best part of my day was:

_____

Today I learned:

_____

Today I want to pray for:

_____

I thank God today for:

_____

Tomorrow I will do the following:

_____

I Protect My Beliefs

Do not be misled. Bad company corrupts good character.
1 Corinthians 15:13 (NIV)

I have stood up for myself in the following ways when someone has wanted me to do something I wasn't comfortable doing:

_____

_____

_____

_____

_____

_____

_____

It's a nice summer day and my best friend's cousin Jamie just came to visit from out of town. The two of them invite me to go to the movies. I am so excited because my favorite movie is playing and I can't wait to meet Jamie that I've heard so much about all year. I ask my mom if I can go and if she can drop me off at the local theater. My mom agrees to drop me off at 3pm and pick me up at 5pm when the movie is over. When my friend and Jamie arrive, Jamie proposes that we ditch the movie and go have some "real fun." When I ask Jamie what "real fun" is, Jamie says, " _____

_____

_____."

There is no way I am ever doing that! This is what I do to get out of the situation:

_____

_____

_____

_____

_____

Jamie calls me a scared baby and doesn't want to hang out with me so I decide to:

_____

_____

_____

_____

_____

Today's date:

_____

Today I am feeling:

_____

The best part of my day was:

_____

Today I learned:

_____

Today I want to pray for:

_____

I thank God today for:

_____

Tomorrow I will do the following:

_____

I Am My Own Person

If sinners entice you, do not give in to them.
Proverbs 1:10 (NIV)

Peer pressure is pressure from peers (friends and people my age around me) to behave and act in a manner similar or acceptable to them. Being under peer pressure is when a peer group wants me to act or do things like them that I may or may not want to do in order to be accepted.

This is how I respond to peer pressure:

_____

_____

_____

_____

_____

_____

This is what I do to stand out from others:

_____

_____

_____

_____

_____

_____

Sometimes I feel peer pressure in school or in other social circles, like on sports teams, in music, dance, or in church in this way:

———————————————————————————————

———————————————————————————————

———————————————————————————————

———————————————————————————————

———————————————————————————————

This is what happened in my life today:

———————————————————————————————

———————————————————————————————

Today's date:

_____

Today I am feeling:

_____

The best part of my day was:

_____

Today I learned:

_____

Today I want to pray for:

_____

I thank God today for:

_____

Tomorrow I will do the following:

_____

I Know God Listens to Me

Those who seek the Lord lack no good thing.
Psalms 34:10b NRSV

My prayers have been answered before when I prayed for the following things for the following reasons:

_____

_____

_____

_____

The prayer below is what I want to ask God to bless my family and me with.

Dear Lord,

I come to you under the power of the Holy Spirit and in the name of your Son Jesus Christ, Lord hear my prayer. I pray for

_____

_____

_____

_____

_____

In Jesus's name, I thank you for answering my prayers.
Amen.

Today's date:

_____

Today I am feeling:

_____

The best part of my day was:

_____

Today I learned:

_____

Today I want to pray for:

_____

I thank God today for:

_____

Tomorrow I will do the following:

_____

I Express Myself Wonderfully with Art, Music, and Dance

Sing to him, sing praise to him: tell of all his wonderful acts.
1 Chronicles 15:16 NIV

I love to do these things most when I am not in school, watching television, or playing video games:

_____

_____

_____

_____

_____

I can see myself making a career of what I love to do as an adult if I continue to:

_____

_____

_____

_____

_____

This is what happened in my life today:

_____

_____

Today's date:

_____

Today I am feeling:

_____

The best part of my day was:

_____

Today I learned:

_____

Today I want to pray for:

_____

I thank God today for:

_____

Tomorrow I will do the following:

_____

I Am Bold Like Jesus

Jesus is described as "The Lamb of God who takes away the sin of the world" in John 1:29. Jesus is also known as The Lion of the tribe of Judah" (Revelation 5:5 NIV).

Here is my explanation of how Jesus could be a vulnerable lamb and also a mighty lion:

_____

_____

_____

_____

_____

_____

_____

If I could be any animal I would choose to be this animal because:

_____

_____

_____

If I could spend a day in the life as this animal I would escape the human world by going and doing:

_____

_____

Today's date:

_____

Today I am feeling:

_____

The best part of my day was:

_____

Today I learned:

_____

Today I want to pray for:

_____

I thank God today for:

_____

Tomorrow I will do the following:

_____

There are No Boundaries When I Believe In Christ

I can do all things through Christ who strengthens me.
Philippians 4:13

I have just become an astronaut and my first mission is to visit the planet _____ to see if there is any life form living there.

I load up with my crew aboard the US _____(name of space shuttle) and spend _____days in outer space on my way to_____ (planet).

When I land and disembark the shuttle, the first thing I see is _____. I am eager to explore.

This is what I find:

_____

_____

_____

_____

_____

_____

_____

Today's date:

_____

Today I am feeling:

_____

The best part of my day was:

_____

Today I learned:

_____

Today I want to pray for:

_____

I thank God today for:

_____

Tomorrow I will do the following:

_____

I Always Represent Myself As a Child of God

Don't you know that you yourselves are God's temple
and that God's Spirit lives in you?
1 Corinthians 3:16 (NIV)

When I wear _____ I feel powerful.

My favorite hairstyle that gives me confidence is _____.

When I play _____ I am in control.

When I am feeling sad I go to _____.

I feel most misunderstood when _____.

If I could express myself in any way to Mom, I would say,

"_____."

If I could say anything to Dad, I would say,

"_____."

If I could change one thing about the world, I would change

_____.

If I could take back one thing I did, it would be

_____.

What I love most about writing is

_____ .

What I love most about myself is

_____ .

The things I am most thankful for in life are

_____ .

My heroes are

_____ .

Today's date:

_____

Today I am feeling:

_____

The best part of my day was:

_____

Today I learned:

_____

Today I want to pray for:

_____

I thank God today for:

_____

Tomorrow I will do the following:

_____

Belief in God is my Foundation

*Trust in the Lord with all your heart, and lean
not on your own understanding; In all your ways
acknowledge Him, and He shall direct your paths.*
Proverbs 3:5-6 (NIV)

My favorite scripture is:

_____

_____

_____

My favorite dinner prayer is:

_____

_____

_____

My favorite bedtime prayer is:

_____

_____

_____

_____

Today's date:

_____

Today I am feeling:

_____

The best part of my day was:

_____

Today I learned:

_____

Today I want to pray for:

_____

I thank God today for:

_____

Tomorrow I will do the following:

_____

I Can Escape Within My Dreams

The Lord is faithful, who will establish you
and guard you from the evil one."
2 Thessalonians 3:3 (NIV)

I come home from school exhausted and decide to take a nap before starting my homework. I fall asleep, and in my dream an angel appears to me. The angel tells me that I can travel with him/her to heaven. I am excited because I always wanted to know if there really was a heaven, but I am kind of scared that I may not return. My angel assures me that he/she will protect and guide me. I take his/her hand, and we both fly out the window and disappear into the sky. The first person I see in heaven is
_____ . I am so overwhelmed with joy that I can go and see anyone in history and in my family that has gone on to heaven. This is what it is like, who all I visit, and what I say to each loved one and hero:

_____

_____

_____

_____

_____

_____

_____

_____

Today's date:

_____

Today I am feeling:

_____

The best part of my day was:

_____

Today I learned:

_____

Today I want to pray for:

_____

I thank God today for:

_____

Tomorrow I will do the following:

_____

I Control My Power and Create My Own Destiny

Let nothing be done through selfish ambition or conceit, but in lowliness of mind let each esteem others better than himself. Let each of you look out not only for his own interest, but also for the interests of others.
Philippians 2:3-4 (NIV)

"_____ (your name)! Wake up! You're going to be late for school," mom yells up the stairs. I jump up, throw on_____, run downstairs to eat

_____, grab my backpack, kiss my parents, and head out the door. On my way to the corner to wait for the bus, I spot something shiny creating a rainbow reflection on the ground. I look around to see where the object could be that is creating this rainbow across my footpath. I look to the right and spot something round and shiny in the street next to the gutter. I go over to inspect the shiny object, and it appears to be a gold coin. I pick it up and put it in my pocket. My bus comes, and I run to jump on. I forget the coin is in my pocket until I get to school, sit at my desk, and stick my hand in my pocket. I start to imagine where it may have come from. I wonder if it has magical powers but I have no time to daydream, because I have to focus in class.

_____ (teacher's name) says, "Everyone clear your desks. We are having a pop quiz on the continents and the countries within them." Oh great, I think to myself sarcastically, because I am not prepared for this test. As my teacher passes out the test, I rub my coin with anxiety. Instantly my worry goes away, and all the answers come to me. I finish the test in fifteen minutes! I then exchange papers with my neighbor to grade tests, and I am the only person in the class that gets 100! I go on having a wonderful day, and I think to myself, I wonder if this coin has magic powers? I decide to test it again. I wish for my favorite hot lunch, the super-duper, big slice of pizza (not the little, hard, circled, round one). I think to myself, There is no way we will have pizza day today, because it is not Friday, and pizza day is only on Friday…but let's see what happens. I walk into the cafeteria, and there is a huge sign that says: "Giant slice pizza will be served today, because our meatloaf machine is broken." I can't believe it! I didn't even know there was a such thing as a meatloaf machine! I'm convinced that my coin is magic. I'm eager to make another wish—but wait! What if this is like the magic genie in a bottle story where I get three wishes, and I only have one wish left? I think long and hard. I decide to wish for _____

because I want it help me_____, but when my wish came true, it caused all kinds of chaos! I had to get rid of it fast and get my life back to normal. This is what I did:

_____

_____

_____

_____

_____

_____

_____

_____

_____

_____

_____

_____

_____

Today's date:

_____

Today I am feeling:

_____

The best part of my day was:

_____

Today I learned:

_____

Today I want to pray for:

_____

I thank God today for:

_____

Tomorrow I will do the following:

_____

I Can Escape My World Through Writing

You are the light of the earth.
Matthew 5:14 (NIV)

This is what I love most about writing:

_____

_____

_____

_____

Writing gives me the freedom to become anything I want to be and love these things about myself:

_____

_____

_____

_____

I am able to escape when I write and realize I am thankful for these things:

_____

_____

_____

I show my appreciation to God for blessing me with an incredible mind and body to imagine and create by:

_____

_____

_____

This is what happened in my life today:

_____

_____

_____

Today's date:

_____

Today I am feeling:

_____

The best part of my day was:

_____

Today I learned:

_____

Today I want to pray for:

_____

I thank God today for:

_____

Tomorrow I will do the following:

_____

I Enjoy Spending Time with My Family

...I thank my God through Jesus Christ for you... Romans 1:8 NLT

It's Friday! Tonight is movie night and I can't wait to pick out the movie I will watch with my family. I am so excited to see the new movie "Stranded" where _____'s (favorite pop star) private plane has to make an emergency landing on what the crew thinks is a deserted island. I can't wait to see how they get off the island, if there are wild creatures living there, or if someone comes to rescue them. I get my popcorn, drink, pop in the movie, fight with my little _____(sibling) over space next to Mom, and the movie begins. I can't believe what happens:

_____

_____

_____

_____

_____

_____

_____

_____

_____

Today's date:

_____

Today I am feeling:

_____

The best part of my day was:

_____

Today I learned:

_____

Today I want to pray for:

_____

I thank God today for:

_____

Tomorrow I will do the following:

_____

A Note to Self

I am the most unique, talented, beautiful person in the world. I will believe in myself, trust my thoughts, and listen to God while obeying my parents. The guided journal stops here, but I will continue writing every day and creating my own stories. Who knows? I may one day write a book, produce a movie, be a songwriter, or a poet, and it all started with journaling. What stories will I continue to create on the following blank pages to make the pages come alive?

_____

_____

_____

_____

_____

_____

_____

_____

_____

_____

_____

_____

_____

_____

CPSIA information can be obtained at www.ICGtesting.com
Printed in the USA
LVOW09s2203201014

409711LV00014B/310/P

9 781613 469910